THE SILENT STRUT OF THE
SHADOW
WARRIOR

My Journey to Inner Strength and Spirit

KAREN TAYLOR

I0459580

SYNERGY
PUBLISHING GROUP

BELMONT, NORTH CAROLINA

The Silent Strut of the Shadow Warrior:
My Journey to Inner Strength and Spirit
Karen Taylor

Published by Synergy Publishing Group,
Belmont, NC
formatting by Melisa Graham

Softcover **ISBN** 978-1-960892-40-9
E-book **ISBN** 978-1-960892-41-6

Dedication

I dedicate this book to my Shadow Warrior, my inner self who is the connection to the Divine. She has held me up and strengthened me throughout my life. I also dedicate it to the women in my ancestry so far back that it is untraceable, the ones from whom I draw my power. Finally, I dedicate this book to any woman who needs to know that she is never alone and has the ability to recognize her own Shadow Warrior.

OTHER WORKS BY KAREN TAYLOR

Learning to Respect my Strut: My Journey as a
Woman Warrior

Unveiling the Secrets: An Encyclopedia by
Women for Women (and those who love them)

Capturing the In-Between: A Collection of Stories
From Empowering Women About Navigating
Here, There, and Everywhere In-Between

Unveiling the Secrets of Being Too
Much: Finally Taking Up Space

CONTENTS

DEAR READER

IN MY FIRST BOOK, *Learning to Respect My Strut: My Journey as a Woman Warrior*, I told of the incident in a fight with a drug dealer where I was injured and how it affected my seven-year-old son. His reaction caused me to remember the terror I saw on his face when I walked into the house with torn, grimy clothes and my arm in a sling. I didn't want him to be afraid every day I went to work as a police officer. And I didn't want to wake up one day realizing I had lost all of his childhood to weird hours and too much time away from home. I also had a big problem with the crowd that surrounded me as I was arresting my suspect. I was doing my job—protecting and serving—and the crowd helped the dealer escape. I couldn't seem to get over that. After a couple of months, I made the decision to leave the police department.

It was not an easy decision. After all, it had been my dream for a long time; I was walking away from it, and I struggled with myself in making the right choice. Nevertheless, I resigned from the police department for my family and … for myself. I felt something else was calling me, but it took many, many years to find that deep-seated desire and bring it out into the sunlight. My Shadow Warrior, a different kind of warrior, was whispering to me. Our Shadow Warriors are our support and our backup when we lose touch with our inner strength and power.

When I left the police department, I thought I lost my strut for a while, but after reflecting, I realized the silent strut of the Shadow Warrior was what sustained me. I had to embark on a journey to find my Shadow Warrior and learn to assert my inner strut. Most of us go through life not realizing we have a Shadow Warrior. We learn this through beliefs and lessons, often passed on through others, that make us believe we have no power over our lives; we are sinners, victims, etc., and we just have to take it on the chin and push through. It took me a long time to really begin to claim my power by acknowledging my Shadow Warrior.

In many ways, this book is presented as a reflection. As you read about my journey, notice each chapter of my personal story will be followed by a section reflecting on how my Shadow Warrior helped me through that time, despite sometimes not being fully aware of her during that specific period in my life. I hope that as I share my journey, you too reflect on your own, noticing and getting to know your own versions of a Shadow Warrior. In sharing my moments of fear and doubt, I have learned to see the "strut" *in* the power of my Shadow Warrior. I hope that you will be encouraged to face your own fears and doubts as a pathway to conquer them. But most importantly, I hope this book supports you in climbing your own personal mountains and shouting from the top, "Here I am, me and my Strut. We are not going anywhere, world, so get used to it."

1

THE SHADOW WARRIOR: THE SILENT STRUT

THE SHADOW WARRIOR is that strongest part of a person's being that waits in the shadows to assist. The Shadow Warrior holds us up, picks us up, surrounds us with protection, and reminds us of our divine nature and power to overcome obstacles and perceived blocks obstructing our paths to our dreams and desires. The battle for which the Shadow Warrior is equipped is the hardest one. She helps us overcome our limiting beliefs and become who we were meant to be. Because of this, she is the strongest warrior ever.

The Shadow Warrior holds no judgment for us; therefore, she holds no judgment for anyone because she knows we are all one. We are all one with the All-That-Is, our Creator, whatever name any of us assigns to her. We have individual personalities, but we are all from the same Spirit. We are the Divine incarnate, and women are the hope of the future. The Divine Feminine is what will save Earth and humanity. The Divine Feminine is wise and old as eternity. That is why we are feared, because of our deep power, and the Shadow Warrior holds that deepest of deep powers.

The Shadow Warrior's purpose is convincing us of our own power and opening our eyes to the fact that we are not victims, if we choose not to be. We go through things in our lives that seem to have occurred outside of our control, but the Shadow Warrior can open our eyes to other ways of perceiving these occurrences.

Though our culture does not reflect the view that peace, love, and compassion are the strongest attributes, it is true nevertheless. The Shadow Warrior is powerful in loving us with compassion, yet firm in demonstrating to us that our choices are our own. Peace comes from accepting ourselves for who we are and having that confident, silent strut of assurance in our value and worthiness. This acceptance is in direct opposition to the dominant belief systems that have convinced us that, as women, we should be small, quiet, nonconfrontational, acquiescent, kind, pretty, nice, and accommodating to whatever the patriarchal, oppressive system assigns as our roles in this life. These belief systems often try to tell us what and how we should eat, what we should and should not wear, where we can go, who we can have a relationship with, and that because we were born with a vagina and not a penis, we aren't supposed to be paid as much as our dick-swinging brothers.

The Shadow Warrior knows that we will get where we need to be, no matter what. She also knows that we sometimes make things harder on ourselves than necessary and that we are learning. This is when she quietly counsels us, if we will listen to her.

My Shadow Warrior is female; however, because she knows all humans, and can encompass both feminine and masculine energy, she chooses to appear to us according to our personal preferences and personalities. She appears to me as a warrior who is stronger than any obstacle or situation I face. She and I have gotten to know each other a little better because I finally started listening to her. I started understanding when she was speaking to me when I was in my late forties. It happened gradually and mostly without my being aware of her during those times of grief and pain, but when I entered my late forties and early fifties, I began to recognize her. She has carried me through it all, and she is so strong that I now know that I can face anything because of her.

The Shadow Warrior is the representation of everything we can be when we reach enlightenment, and that is also a very personal process and a very personal one as individualized as each of us. What I mean by enlightenment is the realization that we are all more than this physical body. We are spirits inhabiting physical bodies. I am not getting into religion here. I just mean that we are souls inhabiting these physical bodies to do whatever it is that we wished to do when we set forth on this journey. Once we reach that realization, we are empowered because we know that we can achieve our dreams.

We are all one, but we are all individualized parts of the one, here to express ourselves in whatever ways we choose. The Shadow Warrior is our support and our backup when we lose touch with our inner strength and power.

2

BILLY SEES MY SHADOW WARRIOR BEFORE I DO

I WAS STILL WORKING on a special team for the police department, and our beat included the housing complexes for lower income families. It was 1994, and the demographics were such that most of the residents were living below the poverty line, and with that came the drug dealing, alcoholism, and domestic violence that can sometimes pervade poverty. Even though drugs, alcoholism, and domestic violence occur in all socioeconomic classes, the privilege that comes with money can keep all of that hidden, so cops mostly deal with those in poverty, those who can't cover their mistakes and avoid getting caught.

The environment I often worked in as a police officer provided my ex-husband an opportunity to attempt to use my job as a means of saying I wasn't taking care of my son. It was bullshit, but he knew that was where he could hurt me because my boy meant everything to me. My sergeant understood that he was using that as a maneuver to try to get full custody and allowed me to take a day shift. One very important thing I have learned is that bad things happen to us, and they will often turn out for the best if we can hold on to that belief and trust the journey. If I hadn't changed shifts, I probably wouldn't have had the opportunity to meet and talk with Billy like I did. It was a blessing in disguise.

Changing shifts was really hard for me because I no longer was able to do special teams operations, and I missed the guys, but my son came first. At any rate, at the end of each shift, I parked my car in the back lot behind the fire department that was situated in the basement of City Hall. The police department was on the top floor of the same building, and the jail was at the back of the first floor behind the courtroom and offices for the public.

I walked past the fire department on my way back to the squad room, and sometimes, some of the firemen would be out back smoking. In those days, you could smoke outside the building. I smoked then, so I would stop and shoot the shit and talk to the guys I knew.

Billy was standing out there with a guy I had gone through training with, and we all just laughed and had a good time. One day, Billy asked if I would like to go out to dinner sometime. It was a little awkward for me because he asked me in front of the other guys, but I told him yes. Later, I told my best friend, Margaret, who was also going through a divorce (being a cop, especially a female cop, is hard on marriages) that I had changed my mind, and I wasn't going to go out with him when he called. She told me to "just go out with him for Pete's sake." She said, "It's not like you're going to marry him." We laughed about that for years, especially since she stood up with me when Billy and I did get married.

Our first date was a trip to Grandfather Mountain in North Carolina. We went in August, but on the top of Grandfather Mountain, it is always much colder than everywhere else, and my sleeveless top and shorts weren't getting the job done, so I bought a sweatshirt from the gift shop. I still have that sweatshirt.

We went on a Saturday, and when we got back to my house, he asked me out for the next day to Hendersonville, North Carolina, because we could have dinner and a drink there. No alcohol sales were legal in the town where we lived at the time because of the blue laws. That day, when Billy picked me up and opened the car door for me, three roses were on the passenger seat. He said they represented the first date because he had a great time, the second date because he was glad I said yes, and the third rose represented his hope for a third date.

My Shadow Warrior was there, but I wasn't recognizing her or her help. Every time I began something new or started down a different path, she was always there, blazing the trail, waiting for me to grasp her hand so she could help me progress forward. She put Billy in my path from my patrol unit to the squad room at the end of my shifts so we could meet.

After Billy and I dated a few times, he told me he would like to take me and my son out to dinner. He wanted to interact with my boy. That just showed the kind of man he was. After we went out, he complimented me on how well-behaved and polite my son was. My son has always made me proud, and to this day, I am still proud of him. He loved his father, and I made sure not to allow my disagreements with his father to become a part of our conversations. No matter what our problems had been, my son was not going to be pulled in two directions. I saw too many children suffer from parents who used them as bargaining chips, and my son was not going to be used that way.

That said, it took my son some time to truly accept Billy, but he did, and I think that is because Billy didn't push or try to influence him. Billy was just a responsible man in every aspect of his life, and once he and I were married, taking care of us was one of his everyday responsibilities.

We dated for six months before Billy asked me to marry him. That sounds like a really short time to me, then and now, but when you know, you know. And I knew. We got married in March, after I had left the police department, and began our new life together.

Billy was a hard worker. Whenever he came home from his paying job, whether from the fire department or painting houses, he would go into the house, visit the loo, get a sip or two of sweet tea, and then go back outside and work on the yard. He mowed the lawn twice a week, at least, and if it rained a lot, he would mow more as soon as the sun shone. When he wasn't mowing, he was working on the mulched beds, pulling weeds, etc. When that was done, he would wash his truck or my vehicle.

He was always doing something. There were times when I told him he needed to just go sit down and relax. That was a major change from what I had experienced in my previous marriage. If anything got done in that relationship, I either had to do it, or there would be an argument to get anything done, and it was done grudgingly. My previous husband's parents had raised him to have zero responsibility for anything. The grass at that house was either mowed by his father or his sister.

As a firefighter, Billy worked a twenty-four hours on, forty-eight hours off shift. On the forty-eight off from the fire department, he worked as a house painter for years before we met and a couple after we were married. I was glad when he stopped painting and started working part-time at a landscaping business not far from our home because the painting was affecting him badly. I saw him come home from painting many days in which they had used a specific type of primer, and after smelling it all day, he would come home and not be able to eat his dinner, and he usually had a healthy appetite.

The man was ever helpful, but not perfect. Even with all of that work, Billy would offer to go to the store for me to pick up a few groceries. After his first run for a full grocery shopping trip at Walmart, I learned not to have him do that anymore. He came home with a half dozen packs of razors and too many bags to count. I knew he had gotten a lot of things not on the list. When I asked him about it, he said they were on sale and a good deal. I told him a good sale was fine, but not if he went over the grocery budget, so that was the end of that.

From that point forward, I made sure I did the main grocery shopping, but sometimes he would request one of his favorite meals, and I wouldn't have all of the ingredients, so I would take the risk and give him a list, and he would go to the store. One of his favorite meals was fried chicken strips with rice and gravy. Of course, I always made sure we had a green vegetable to go with the Southern-fried chicken strips, brown gravy, and biscuits to make myself feel better about the questionable healthiness of all that fried goodness. The funny part was that I never made enough gravy. Billy and my son would eat every last bite of that gravy each time, and Billy would say, "You need to make more gravy." Finally, I made an entire electric skillet full to the brim with gravy, and no one said I needed to make more.

While not a talented grocery shopper, Billy took care of our vehicles with the precision of a heart surgeon. If I came home and said the car was making an unusual sound, he would immediately go check it out and get it resolved. If he didn't know how to fix it, he always knew someone who could. He was a lot like my dad in that way. Dad always brought my sister and me up to pay attention to our cars. He taught us how to check the oil, radiator, tire pressure, and brake fluid. I knew how to put oil, air, and brake fluid in and helped him with all the vehicles when he needed someone to crank or turn the engine off as he tinkered with them, so I knew from that to let Billy know if something wasn't correct in the car, and Billy appreciated it.

Billy cleaned and detailed our vehicles regularly too. His truck was washed and cleaned inside and out at least twice per week, sometimes three, depending upon the weather. That truck was so clean you could eat off the floors. My car has never been as clean since. I asked him once why he didn't have a detailing business on the side instead of painting all those years because he was so good at it. He responded that no one wanted to pay the price that it was worth and said one of my favorite sayings he would use, "I can sit at home and scratch a broke ass," meaning he wasn't going to work hard at something to be paid less than it was worth.

That is the same reason that he didn't do any paint jobs on his own. He painted for a man who had his own business and set the prices for the jobs himself, so Billy just got paid for his work, and he was paid pretty well because he was a master painter for sure. I remember when he was touching up the baseboards in the kitchen. He didn't use tape or a cloth on the floor or anything. He just laid the paintbrush against those baseboards and smoothly applied the paint, not dripping the first drop on the floor or missing and hitting the wall. It was something to see.

Billy's pickiness extended to the yard, not just the vehicles. The way he mowed the lawn was quite specific. It had to be done a certain way, in a certain direction at the proper height for the cut. He would weed eat with the same precision, and afterward, he would blow the cuttings off the driveway with a blower so loud you could hear it two blocks away.

My dad liked him, and that is another big deal to me because my dad was a damn good judge of character, and he was always my hero. I know that women tend to be that way with their dads, and a lot of times, we unfairly compare our husbands to our dads, and measuring up to my heroic view of my dad was a lot to ask of a man.

Billy loved to fish, so I started going with him to fish sometimes. Bass fishing was his favorite, and we would travel to several area lakes for largemouth bass and stripers. One lake was closer than the others that we would occasionally visit to fish for white bass, but his favorite was the largemouth and stripers. Largemouth bass were always catch and release, but the big lake we fished for stripers allowed a maximum of five fish per person, so we would sometimes bring home some to freeze and later have a fish fry. He made the best homemade tartar sauce. Once, we invited my family over for a fish fry, and my brother-in-law said he didn't like tartar sauce, but he tasted Billy's and ended up eating almost the entire bowl. We all laughed at him for that.

Frying fish and making tartar and cocktail sauce were his culinary gifts. The rest of the cooking he left to me. He loved my cooking, but sometimes he would say something like, "At the fire department, so and so makes it like …," and he would tell me how they did it. After a couple of times of that, I looked at him and said, "This is not the fire department. This is my kitchen, and I will do it my way." Now, just so that doesn't sound like I was being a total asshole, let me give some context.

Since I had been a public safety officer (PSO) for the police department at the same place Billy was a firefighter, I had gone through all the training for fighting fire with some of the firemen Billy had worked with for years. Some of the guys were all right, but a few of them were misogynistic assholes who were not the least bit shy about their feelings concerning women firefighters and police officers. These guys were the ones who had been firemen for years and thought women should stay in their place and that because they were born with a penis, they did anything and everything better than women, including cooking, etc. I had enough interactions with some of these pricks when I had gone through training and afterward, so I wasn't interested in how they did anything. I laid it all out there to Billy. He listened and attempted to rationalize their behavior, but I cut him off. I knew he loved me, but I also knew he would never be able to understand how it felt, because he was a white male. That stayed a point of contention throughout our marriage.

This was just one point of contention among many moments of laughter throughout our relationship. For instance, Billy got along with my sister really well. She has a great sense of humor and was able to joke around with him, and he was a great sport. He really thought a lot of her. I remember one Christmas Eve, the family was at our house for dinner to celebrate. Billy was working, but they let him come home to eat with us. I had candles on the dinner table, and my sister, Jean, was leaning over to help her son with something. She was wearing a decorative Christmas sweater that had gold threads on it, and one of the threads caught on fire. The flame jumped on that thread and ran the length of it up my sister's sweater, and she quickly pulled it off. The fire was out, and we were all reeling from the excitement that only lasted a few seconds.

Jean looked at Billy and said, "You're a fireman. A lotta help you were." Billy never skipped a beat. He just grinned and put a bite of food in his mouth and said, "I'm on break." We all broke out in a fit of even more laughter after the excitement was over. We still tell that story when the family gets together.

Though I may have made Billy sound like a saint up until this point, like most people, he had to eat his words a time or two. For instance, I locked my keys in my car one day, so I had to call him to come open it. He was working at the fire department, but he was at a station that was in close proximity. When he arrived to assist me, he said, "I have never locked my keys up in my car."

I replied, "Well, it's not like I meant to." He said, "You need to pay attention." I think I told him to kiss my ass and went home.

A few weeks went by until one Sunday, Billy was working and called me to bring the extra key to his truck. He had locked his keys inside. I didn't say anything over the phone except, "Okay, I'm on my way." When I walked into the bay at the fire department, Billy started telling me how he accidentally locked his keys in his truck. He was cleaning the inside of it, he said, and the door shut, and his keys were inside. I listened, not responding yet. I just had a smirk on my face. After a few brief moments, I walked over, unlocked his truck, and said, "I thought you never locked your keys in your truck. You need to pay attention." We both laughed, and his sergeant standing nearby laughed too. Everyone knew how picky and anal Billy could be at times, but they all liked him.

Although I knew the dangers of being a firefighter, because I had been a public safety officer and gone through the training, it still didn't keep me from being concerned about Billy's safety. For the most part, I handled it pretty well, but I remember one day, I was home while Billy was on his shift, and I turned on the television and saw a breaking news story. One of the oldest buildings in our town, the train depot, had caught on fire, and the news was covering it. It was a summer day in the South, and the firefighters were being attended by the paramedics because of the heat. Turnout gear is designed to protect firefighters from fire, so the gear they wore added to the heat factor. So, as the guys were taking turns fighting the fire, the ones not engaged were having bags of ice applied to them to keep them from suffering from heat exhaustion.

The camera panned out and showed a lone firefighter on the roof of the building with an ax. Anyone who has seen the full turnout gear knows that there is no way to know who is in the gear because it is bulky and disguises the body shape and characteristics, but I knew from the way that firefighter held his body and wielded the ax, that it was Billy. I stayed glued to that television until the story went off. When Billy and I talked on the phone later, I asked him if that was him on the roof, and he said it was. I knew it was him. He wanted to know how I knew, and I said, "I just knew because I could tell by the way you held your body." He never said it, but I think that meant something to him. Like me, Billy had gone through a couple of failed relationships. He had his own trust issues, and I think my knowing that he was the one on top of the building made him realize the depth of my love for him.

I think he also realized how much I loved him because I was able to understand Billy's relationship with his coworkers because it was similar to the relationship that cops have. When people work together in dangerous situations on the regular, a special bond occurs that is hard for those outside of the professions to grasp. This is true for EMTs, paramedics, and probably nurses in the ER, I would suspect. I think that is one reason Billy and I got along as well as we did, because we had both experienced seeing people in terrible situations, doing terrible things to themselves and others, and when you witness such tragedy and trauma, it changes you.

Another thing that made my marriage work and life better was our sense of humor. Billy and I understood gallows humor. We were able to laugh about almost anything, and one of the things we did well was to trade insults, but in a fun way. Someone who didn't know us might think we hated each other or that we were arguing, but it was our sense of humor developed from a life of being a cop and a firefighter, dealing with the worst of humanity and staying sane by means of humor as a coping mechanism.

My son and his two friends would stand in our living room listening to Billy and me riff on each other, or one of the boys would ask a question they knew would prompt a story from our work experiences. They were good times, and I think back on those days with great affection.

Billy was diagnosed with stage IV lung cancer in May 2006. He lived until the following January before he passed away after ten years together. Those last few months with him were the hardest months of my life. I can't write about that. But, all in all, Billy was a wonderful man, and I still miss him every day, even after seventeen years. Unlike other women and their marriage experiences, I never had to wonder where Billy was. I knew he was there for me. I knew he had my back. I didn't concern myself with him cheating either because he had integrity. He and I had both had tough marriages we had gotten out of, and we understood each other. He was my soulmate, and I doubt there will ever be another.

HELP FROM MY SHADOW WARRIOR

During this period of my life, though I was unaware of my strong Shadow Warrior friend, she assisted me through the changes, and I believe she had a hand in bringing Billy and me together.

I believe, though he most likely couldn't have articulated it, he saw that strength in me that came from my Shadow Warrior. He could see what I couldn't, which was that deep part of me that was learning how to come into who I really am. She made herself known to him so that he and I would come together as we did. She has always had my best interests at heart.

These days, I have a better understanding of why there won't be another romantic partner for me. I did try dating at one point, but I was comparing everyone I met to Billy, and they weren't measuring up. Experiencing a good marriage with my soulmate has been vital to my spiritual growth, and I have developed a deeper relationship with my Shadow Warrior after going through the loss of Billy. I have sat with her on many occasions, just waiting for any wisdom she has to impart. I believe I have chosen to not pursue any more romantic relationships because I am committed to understanding myself at the deepest level I can, and my Shadow Warrior is a part of that deep part of me. To come into a deep understanding of myself is a quest I embrace, and I know that my Shadow Warrior is the part of me that is waiting for the rest of me to catch up to her.

3

FROM COP TO OFFICE: SQUARE PEG IN A ROUND HOLE

EVEN THOUGH I HAD BILLY, I remember feeling that part of my identity was gone because I was no longer a cop. The dream I'd had since I was a kid was over. Could being a wife and mom be enough? I didn't voice these questions to anyone because to me, being a wife and mother possibly not being enough sounded awful. Had I been able to recognize my Shadow Warrior then, I would've realized that what I was afraid of missing was deep inside of me, not outside in a job.

I didn't miss shift work or working holidays, but I missed that feeling of belonging to the crew in blue. I didn't talk about these feelings a lot either because I'd always been one to make a decision and move forward. Little did I know that the feeling of belonging was merely a particle of what I could feel in connecting with my deeper self, my Shadow Warrior.

Not talking about my feelings fit my personality because I had a tendency to suppress things and try to ignore them, but internally, I berated myself, calling myself weak and other names. Over time, I have realized that suppressing things is actually the weak-minded thing to do. The strong thing to do is to face the emotion and deal with it.

If I could go back in time, I would change how I did some things. For one, I would not have left the police department and gone straight into an office environment. Bad idea. Yet, after many years of reflection, I have begun to believe that all life experiences are valuable, even if they sucked at the time I experienced them. This is an important lesson for me. The path I have taken has brought a great deal of life experience and lessons, and I don't regret them. Had I not gone straight into an office environment, I wouldn't have learned many things, the main one being I don't enjoy that setting.

I went from working in an open environment using cars, vans, my feet, and a couple of times, a bicycle, as tools of my job and rolling offices with a bunch of guys and a couple women, to sitting in an office with one guy, the boss, and six other women, whom I felt had very different personality traits than I did. In addition, most people who have no cops in the family have no conception of the jobs we did and how we handled things, especially our gallows humor.

Cops develop a sense of humor that can be considered offensive and inappropriate, but it is a means of handling the stress and ugliness they face each and every day. People outside of the profession usually don't understand. Firefighters, EMTs, and paramedics share the same kind of humor. Being married to Billy was a comfort because he was a firefighter and had been for many years, so he and I shared some of the same tainted, cynical views of the world and its people. However, though he tried, he wasn't a lot of help with my attempt to navigate working with an office full of women as opposed to partners in a platoon at the police department.

I missed some parts of being a cop, like the fun I had with some of the guys as we joked and cut up. I missed being able to work in a larger, open area, not confined to an office, and I missed the adrenaline rush I got sometimes while on the job; I would be a liar if I said I didn't. But I didn't miss a lot of the bullshit we put up with as police officers on the daily, so I guess it balanced out.

I did struggle with tamping down my assertive behavior. I was, and still am, quite blunt at times, and that doesn't always serve me. I have always had a tendency to disdain what I call mamby-pamby, beating around the bush; however, there is a time and a place to be strongly assertive, and I have made progress in that area. I won't say that being an in-your-face, brutally honest person is a characteristic of the Shadow Warrior because a warrior knows when to speak and when to be silent. Had I been more in touch with my Shadow Warrior, I would've learned to watch my mouth more often, and if I couldn't say something helpful, I would've held my counsel.

I missed being a cop and the camaraderie I had with my coworkers. This camaraderie is very similar to what soldiers experience when they face dangers together. I know now that leaving the police department was essential, not only for my son, but for my future endeavors of which I had no inkling. My Shadow Warrior self knew what was coming, so she urged me through my gut feelings to do what I did. I wish I had listened more carefully because there were times I didn't and ended up going the long way around the journey, but then again, I think that was part of the process.

When I left the police department I faced a new beginning, a new marriage, a nine-to-five office job, and no direction for my purpose. As a member of an all-female staff, I got to experience a monster-dose of stereotypical female behavior all at once. That was an eye-opener. I knew from being a woman how treacherous we females can be, but I hadn't thought about it or experienced it in such a large dose for a long time, probably since high school.

Two women in this office were at the top of the food chain. One was the administrative assistant to the boss who did all the non-real estate work such as wills, estate planning, bookkeeping, legal correspondence, etc. The other one was the head real estate secretary. Though these two women had worked together for this attorney for years, they still periodically gossiped about each other, so the gossip and backstabbing floated downhill and pervaded the rest of the staff.

A fair amount of backstabbing occurred in the police department, but since I wasn't interested in gaining rank or moving up, I was able to avoid a lot of that. Sexual innuendos and comments were mostly what I dealt with, and though that was annoying, for some reason, I found that having women gossip about me behind my back and act like they were friends to my face was much more difficult to handle.

Looking back now, I recognize that this type of behavior is pretty common, and I think it arises from some of the stereotypes about women that have been perpetuated over time. If we women can recognize and respect our own *strut*, we will have no need for backstabbing. We can support each other and help each other out.

No longer did I have to work third shift and then go to court the next morning, but the attorney I worked for did a lot of real estate closings. My time in his office was during the boom of refinances that began in the 1990s (and by 2008, though I was long gone, these refinances ended up a disaster as evidenced by the movie *The Big Short*). This attorney's goal was one hundred closings per month with four closing secretaries, a courier, an administrative assistant, and a receptionist (me) who opened files, answered four phone lines, made copies, and whatever else was needed in the pandemonium of closings per month. There was also a title insurance specialist who took care of the files after the closings.

Closings traditionally happened on the last two or three days of every month because of per diem costs, so they included new home purchases and refinances. We did many more refinances, but there were still a lot of purchases. Those last three days of the month were hell. The days ran from 8:00 a.m. to 6:00 p.m. and sometimes later because there was always something that didn't work out as planned. I got to a point where I hated my job there.

To give an idea of how focused this attorney was on moving people quickly through his office, he made sure he kept the air conditioning on year-round. His secretaries froze at their desks, wearing sweaters and running little space heaters underneath their desks. Some of his male clients were known to sarcastically ask if our boss had forgotten to pay the heating bill. I am usually pretty good with cooler temperatures, but I was at a desk directly underneath a vent, and I even got cold. Realtors would come in and complain about the temperatures, and when no one but the office staff was around, he would say, "That's a good way to keep people from hanging around talking after the closings. If they're cold, they will leave faster." He wanted those closings moving along as fast as possible, and he didn't want to spend a lot of time answering questions. And, honestly, I didn't want to spend a lot of time in that environment, so I soon decided to leave.

One of my husband's high school buddies was also an attorney, and he was looking for an office assistant, so I ended up going to work for him. The amount of closings were fewer, but it was stressful for other reasons. For one, his office manager and he had a weird personality dynamic going on. They had been together, just the two of them, since he'd graduated law school, and they were used to one another. Having a new person come into the office was a big adjustment for them, and I had to learn an entirely new personality dynamic.

In retrospect, the truth of the matter was that I was a round peg trying to fit into a square hole, and I didn't fit very well at all. During the time I was trying to fit myself into the square hole of a traditional office environment, I was navigating being a civilian, raising my son, and adapting to combined family life. I had relatively normal working hours, I was there for my son more often, I had to buy a wardrobe because I no longer wore a uniform, we had dinner together on the nights Billy wasn't at the fire department, and we worked on the house and the yard together. Life had its ups and downs, but Billy and I were happy, and I knew I had made the right decision leaving the force, marrying him, and pursuing a different career path. Life went on, my son entered high school, and Billy and I did fun things together.

HELP FROM THE SHADOW WARRIOR

During this period of my life, I was struggling with my identity. I felt I had lost touch with an important part of who I was, and unfortunately, I struggled mostly in silence because I didn't think I had the right to struggle or complain. I had a loving, supportive husband, and my son was healthy and whole. Initially, I was unaware of my Shadow Warrior's help during this phase of my life. Looking back now, I know that she helped me to just show up and do the inner work, even when I hated it. She helped me to focus on my family and to begin building a life outside of work.

4

THE GYM: COPING

THE GYM HAS PLAYED an important part in my life. I always knew that I felt invigorated after a good sweat session, but I now recognize how I used working out, not only as a means of coping with stress, but as a means of fighting my inner dialogue about my weight, body image, self-worth, and the aging process.

I became quite the gym rat, and it was to the point of obsession. Working out helped me build strength and confidence in some ways. But in certain moments, my inner voice, which I called "my Monster Bitch," became dominant, and the gym environment allowed more space for the Monster Bitch (MB) to grow ever stronger in her diatribe of detrimental dialogue. The Monster Bitch focused on the negative beliefs I had always had about my body. Despite the fact that I was doing something positive for myself, the MB still found ways to focus on the parts of my body that were slower to respond to the diet and exercise. On days when I felt tired, she would berate me, calling me lazy and fat, etc., so I didn't miss many workouts at all, and thankfully the endorphins I experienced from them would usually drown out the MB's voice.

Some of the positive ways the gym helped me was in affording me a space of activity and the ability to focus on building muscle and drowning out the distracting things in life that sapped my energy. Distracting things like what people thought of me, the uncomfortable feeling of working in an office full of women, trying to fit into the office environment, silly personal dramas, etc. Working out was meditation for me, but thoughts of working out and dieting overtook a lot of my thoughts during the day. Even though eating, sleeping, and breathing fitness, metaphorically, is quite common among people who are, like myself at the time, preparing for bodybuilding contests, and even though it had its place in my journey, I recently recognized that I used that lifestyle to navigate leaving the police department and developing an identity outside of the force.

Because of the dreariness of working in the attorney's office, I wanted to chase the dream of doing a bodybuilding contest. It was a new adventure to pursue, but I also became rather obsessed with working out and eating the bodybuilding diet. It made me feel good about myself in a lot of ways because I looked at it as a painter or sculptor does when they create a work of art, only I was doing it with my body. However, my goal to compete in bodybuilding also supported the old negative body image voice in my head as I became obsessed with grams of protein, carbohydrates, fat, and the balance of that with the workouts. Those old beliefs that I wasn't skinny enough, pretty enough, etc. turned into negative thoughts about how I was doing with my bodybuilding journey. I would hear a voice tell me that I didn't have enough muscle tone in the triceps, I ate too many carbs yesterday, not enough vascularity, not enough water today, and more. But bodybuilding also fulfilled my desire to be strong and overcome obstacles. While I wrestled with some of the negative thoughts, a new set of beliefs were forming at the same time, a burgeoning belief that my body was fine whether I decided to bodybuild or not. Indeed, that time in my life served me, and I still think working out is helpful in so many ways. But now, I recognize that working out and dieting, like anything else in life, should be balanced.

Each week, Monday through Friday, I was up at 4:20 a.m. I drove to the gym, worked out, came home, got my son up for school, saw Billy off to work, got myself ready for work, and dropped my son off on my way into the office. On Tuesdays and Thursdays after work, I returned to the gym for boot camp class, and I attended this class again on Saturday mornings. I was working out six days a week and twice on Tuesdays and Thursdays. I know this helped me as I navigated a new way of life, one without the camaraderie of the guys in the police department, because the boot camp group became a good substitute. We worked out together, laughed, and commiserated about diets, etc., and how other people didn't understand us and our goals. This is similar to the "us against them" belief we all had as cops. I didn't realize it at the time, but in retrospect, I recognize I was transferring the old cop squad for a new squad of exercisers. I felt a sense of belonging with that boot camp group that I never felt in the office work that I did. Both the boot camp sessions and my individual workouts took up a lot of my time, but it was a way of getting through some things I didn't even realize I was working through.

Billy was understanding through it all, and his being as responsible a person as he was made it easier for me to chase this dream. He helped me by being there for my son in the afternoons when I was working out, but I always came home and cooked dinner and did all the things women are expected to do when they work and have families. I had the gym, and he had his fishing, so we made our outside interests fit and our marriage work.

Though we made things work, it was far from easy. For instance, when I cooked regular meals for my family, I also had to cook special meals for myself in order to follow my bodybuilding guidelines. It was labor intensive on many levels, and I realized much later in life that during that period of my life, I was staying "filled-up and busy" so that I didn't have to think and feel as much.

All in all, even though I know it took time away from my family, I know my son was proud of my efforts. He didn't come out and say so, but I could tell by little things he did and said that he was proud. Even though Billy never truly understood why I wanted to do bodybuilding, he would say to me sometimes, "I wish I had your drive," so I know that, in his own way, he was proud of me as well. And I was proud of myself.

HELP FROM MY SHADOW WARRIOR

That "drive" he talked about is something I still have, not always, but some of the time. I now know that another name for it is my "strut," and it is facilitated by my Shadow Warrior, who is always in the background holding me up when I falter. As I have matured, I realize that the Shadow Warrior and the strut are interrelated. Actually, they could be described as two facets of the same being. Two parts of the inner me that are working together in concert.

I envision her standing behind me in those workouts shouting encouragement. My idea of a powerful female warrior, a true Amazon, has always been there in the back of my mind. Times when I was pushing myself toward a new goal in weight training, or times when I had to face something incredibly difficult, that image has been there, and I know my Shadow Warrior truly exists.

5

PERIMENOPAUSE

As I WAS SPENDING so much time at the gym, pursuing my dream of doing a bodybuilding contest, I began experiencing perimenopausal symptoms at the relatively early age of thirty-nine. During this time, there wasn't a lot of information about perimenopause, and the little that was out there received derisive snorts from a great many doubters. Fortunately for me, Billy wasn't one of the snorters. He listened to me and saw the kind of physical symptoms I began having, like sudden hot flashes that felt like someone stuck a hot poker to my back with the heat radiating from there throughout my body, or sweats that, despite being used to sweaty workouts, reached an entirely new level of swamp ass, irritability and mood swings (which caused some people to suggest I was taking anabolic steroids when I most certainly was not), and erratic periods. This was a big indicator that I was perimenopausal because my periods had always been as regular as clockwork.

I know that working out like I did probably helped me with the mood swings because perimenopause brought irrational rages. My time in the gym and that physical activity probably saved me from completely snapping a few times, but I still had times where I couldn't hide my rage and people continued to make comments about anabolic steroids. In those days, there was even less information about perimenopause than today, so that explains some people's belief that I was using steroids. The lack of information about perimenopause paired with common cultural expectations of women did not do me any favors. For example, one common belief is that women aren't supposed to get angry, and if they do, they aren't supposed to show it. If they do, they are called crazy. Men can get angry and punch walls, but women aren't supposed to. We are supposed to be nice, kind, and quiet. If we need to deal with our emotions, there is a perception for some that the only acceptable way to do so is to cry quietly and prettily so that we can be comforted by our men. I call bullshit on that one. Fortunately, my husband was more evolved in a lot of ways than many other men I knew.

One day, I got home, and Billy told me about a television show he had watched with a doctor, Christiane Northrup, who specialized in women's health. He told me that she had written a book about perimenopause. It made me see that Billy wanted to help me feel better and that he was honoring my love of books and reading. This made me love him more because it showed me that he listened to me and had paid attention to who I was. I ordered the book and read it, and it helped some. But the more important lesson I learned from that book was how much my husband loved me.

I remember one day while at work, I was on a phone call with someone. I can't remember the issue, but I know it was a problem, and I became frustrated. I also got hot and stood up, took off the button up shirt I was wearing over another top, and flung it on the floor. My coworker's eyes got quite big, but she didn't say anything. She was then and still is a perceptive woman, so I think she could see that I was having a hot flash on top of a frustrating phone conversation. Despite her perceptive nature, she was still shocked at my reaction. I don't blame her. It is our culture. Again, women are expected to present a certain persona to the world, and if we deviate from that, we are called all the names. We see it all the time in the news media: crazy, bitch, out of control, domineering, and the list goes on. If we act outside of those cultural beliefs, we are punished for acting outside of the accepted behavioral norms.

So, in addition to dealing with the hormonal fluctuations of perimenopause and the seeming loss of control of ourselves, I still had to deal with antiquated belief systems based upon rules written in obsolescence without consideration of the changes that the passage of time brings. These belief systems are based upon a patriarchal system with its foundation in religion that serves to keep women oppressed. I have been around plenty of people who will quote biblical passages that lay out the expectations for women's behavior. These rules in the Bible were written during a time when women were considered chattel or property, like cattle or other material items. Women had no rights. They couldn't own property or anything like that. While I was experiencing extreme changes in my body, it was infuriating to think I was still supposed to adhere to a doctrine that originated in an era that viewed me, a woman, merely as property.

Additionally, the health care system and society have only begun to recognize the unique health concerns like those that occur in perimenopause and menopause. Our culture still has a long way to go to bring things to the level they should be in treating women's health issues. We've only recently, within the last couple of decades, begun openly discussing things like menstruation, perimenopause, and menopause. I remember when I was a young girl watching *All in the Family,* and the character, Edith, was "going through the change." That is what it used to be called in hushed whispers away from male ears because they didn't need to worry about women's problems. While the shift to more open conversations is happening within my lifetime, which illustrates some degree of progression, there is still much more to accomplish. We no longer have the hushed whispers, but women's healthcare still has a long way to go to be as effective as it should be.

It has taken me a long time to realize that I am naturally powerful and that patriarchal supporters are afraid of my and all women's power. Some of us still don't realize how powerful we are. Some of us think our power lies in the emotional manipulation of those we love in order to get what we want. We commit emotional manipulation of significant others, husbands, partners, children, etc., and when we hit the hellacious roller coaster ride of perimenopause, we do lose some control, but I submit that the loss of control I experienced was necessary to my own personal development. Perimenopause was a marker, like a signboard, showing me the way to becoming more powerful than I ever realized I could. But, it took time to realize these changes were happening *for* me.

I didn't have the wisdom in those days to sit quietly and listen to my body. Years of attempting to force myself into preconceived notions of acceptable behavior for women had separated me from the most important thing: knowing myself through my body. These days, I am better at sitting quietly, but it is still an ongoing process. Instead of sitting quietly in those days, I filled my days with work, the gym, and navigating family life. It wasn't all bad. I had some wonderful times with my family, but because of the belief system I had cultivated since I was a young girl, I struggled a lot. The old body image beliefs I had my entire life were looming even larger because of aging and perimenopause. I was thirty-nine years old. Though I wasn't old, I had all the concerns that assail women regarding aging.

I saw a few wrinkles here and there, but if I could've looked forward to who I am now, I would've seen my current self laughing at my thirty-nine-year-old self worrying about wrinkles. My body was changing, and with that change came the crone wisdom that Clarissa Pinkola Estés talks about in her book, *Women Who Run With Wolves*. However, when facing the concept of a crone at thirty-nine years old, especially from the perspective of the cultural expectations of how women supposedly should look and act, it was daunting and depressing. No woman wants to feel old and unattractive. Now, I'm experiencing a time in my life that I've heard and read about other women my age and older experience: the invisibility of older women. Once a woman reaches a certain age, she is overlooked because she no longer fits into the age bracket of attractiveness. Of course, I realize this is a cultural construct, but it still has a great deal of power. Instead of recognizing the wisdom and power that age brings a woman, our culture projects an idea that her value as a woman decreases with the frequent appearance of more wrinkles and the shifting of body shapes. In other more base wording, a woman's loss of fuckability reduces her value to the patriarchy, and her ability to cook well or other more domestic characteristics become more of a commodity. Once again, I call bullshit. Our "fuckability" can turn to "fuck you and the horse you rode in on" because we are powerful in every way, and our value shouldn't be tied to how well we can attract the male gaze. We can be valuable human beings outside of sexual considerations.

All of this I have said doesn't mean I think older women shouldn't have sex. I think that women should do whatever they damn well please. It should be our choice as to whether or not we engage in intimacy and with whom. It should be completely our choice, not based upon cultural expectations of any kind because as we know, our culture is a patriarchal one. As I write this, we have just last week received the news that the presidential election of 2024 resulted in Trump returning to the White House, alongside J. D. Vance and other privileged white men who are afraid of the power of women. I have seen several social media posts discussing how women and girls have experienced men saying to them, "your body, my choice." It takes a lot of control for me to not say the first thing that comes into my mind as a response to that idiocy, but I am working on myself these days to become the person I wish to be, so suffice it to say that ignorance like that comes from a state of deep fear. In order to combat that fear, I need to remember to protect myself by being strong and not give in to the attempt of outside forces to scare me and other women.

Perimenopause, though I didn't realize it at the time, offered me a time to reflect on myself. However, I didn't do that a lot back then. As I do that very thing now, I realize that perimenopause can be a gift, and it could've gone a helluva lot easier if I had understood more about these things then. Looking back on this time, I now give myself grace and understanding, things I couldn't and didn't give myself at the time. These days, I allow myself to be human and make mistakes. I still beat the shit out of myself at times, but I am getting better at recognizing when I do that to myself, and I stop. If I can't give myself grace, I know I can't give others grace.

As I was navigating all the things, I was also dealing with my son going through puberty and becoming a teenager, so our household had a lot of mood swings, not just mine. I know my husband probably felt like he was living in a war zone at times, but he stayed steady through most of it. Little did I know what was on the horizon.

My body was preparing me for something I would have to face that would damn near destroy me. After I had been experiencing months of intermittent periods, the first week of June 2006, the week of my birthday, Billy was diagnosed with cancer, and I experienced my last period. I've often thought that it was a blessing that my period stopped then, and its ending served a purpose. I could more easily focus on taking care of Billy.

HELP FROM THE SHADOW WARRIOR

This period in my life was fraught with crazy mood swings, raging hormonal changes and self-flagellation because I didn't understand myself at all. Additionally, my son was going through the teenage years and had his own hormonal changes. My Shadow Warrior was there in the background, helping me through some of those times, especially in the gym. I was able to connect with power and strength through training with weights and bolstering my self-esteem because I had felt lost since I left the police department. My Shadow Warrior knew I needed the release of the physical activity, and she knew I wouldn't be satisfied joining a walking group. She knew I needed a stringent program to help me focus on something besides the loss I felt, despite my happy marriage and my beloved son.

Sometimes, when I think about those days, I envision myself working out back then and an image of this beautifully strong, powerful warrior, dressed in battle gear standing behind me as I work out, battle axe raised in the air, shouting encouragement. Of course it is an imagined thing, but it feels very real. No doubt, my Shadow Warrior guided me through this period in my life, and several others.

6

THE SHADOW WARRIOR, LOSS, LOVE, AND MOTHERHOOD

I HAVE ONE BIOLOGICAL SON, but I tell everyone I have three sons because my son and his two best friends, Austen and Kris, spent a lot of time together, splitting their time among the three homes. These three young men taught me a great deal more than I already had learned from working with a bunch of men. They had a younger view, yet there were still cultural stereotypes. They still viewed women as physically weaker and needing their protection as men. They still held on to the belief that women should be the ones who took care of the home, cooked meals, etc. They, like everyone, had been indoctrinated too, but all three were smart and able to see things that amazed me, like their ability to understand my viewpoint of oppression and discrimination sometimes.

The boys had a great respect for me and for Billy, and they loved the humor in our relationship, that humor that is sometimes considered dark humor that cops, firefighters, doctors, nurses, and other professionals that deal with the darker edges of human nature share. The boys would stand around and listen to us and laugh, saying how much they loved coming to our house.

Sometimes, one of my boys would ask a question about something they knew would spark a discussion around being cops and firefighters, so they could listen to our stories. I realized what they were doing, but I was okay with it because I hoped that something Billy and I learned along the way might one day help them. Little did I know what was coming and how much that help would matter.

After Billy died and I was trying to deal with the loss of him, financial stability, and life as I knew it, my son entered the Marine Corps and entered boot camp. I had read everything I could get my hands on about the Marine Corps, especially boot camp. The corps provided some information for family, etc., but I knew that it didn't scrape the surface of a percentage of what went on there.

One book I read, *Into the Crucible* by James B. Woulfe, described the last event that all boot camp recruits had to successfully complete in order to become a Marine. It was eye-opening, and it caused me some concern because of the difficulty of it. I eased my own mind with thoughts of how strong I knew my son was and how much I knew a dream could drive a person's will. It was still hard for me, and any mother will know how difficult it is to release their child and willfully allow them to grow and become an adult in a hard environment. Through it all, my Shadow Warrior was silently helping me.

I had promised my son that I would write to him while he was at boot camp. The recruits were not allowed to have any other communication. They did get to use the phone to call home after they had completed the Crucible, and that was a wonderful moment. During the weeks prior to that call, I wrote him a letter every day he was in boot camp. Every day without fail.

Boot camp lasted thirteen weeks, the longest of any branch in the military. My son told me later that they had not received mail every day, but when they did, he always got a pile all at once, and a couple of the guys asked him where all the letters were from. He just said, "My mama." When he told me that, at first, I thought all of those letters may have caused him to be the target of mocking, especially in such a testosterone-filled environment, but I knew that those letters meant something to him. To be honest, writing them to him every day got me through some very tough days. Additionally, I knew my son was no shrinking violet and was a tough nut to crack. He was and is a warrior in his own right.

Another thing that got me through some tough days was my precious dog, Jake. Billy had gotten me Jake as a gift a couple of years before he died, and that dog and I were inseparable. We went on walks every day, and he was my constant companion. I never left him for very long, and I know that it was more for me than for him because I honestly do not know how I would've made it without him.

Many people helped me get through those times after losing Billy. Included in that group were my other two sons—the ones I didn't birth, but they are still mine. Kris checked on me whenever he wasn't working, and Austen checked on me every day. His mother, Sharon, did too. She and Danny, her husband, were a big help. My mom checked on me regularly too, as well as my sister, but my mom and sister lived in North Carolina, and I was still living about an hour's drive away, give or take. I found out many years later that my son had asked Austen to check on me. I know Austen would've checked on me anyway, but it warmed my heart to know that my son knew I would miss him, and he was probably worried since we had lost Billy the second week of his military boot camp.

All three of my sons graduated high school at the same time, and Austen and Kris were working. They hadn't chosen to attend college yet, but later, Kris did. Austen wanted to go into the Army. His grandfather had served as sergeant major, and Austen held him in high regard. The problem was that the recruiters didn't want to spend their time talking to Austen because he was over the weight limits outlined in their tables. Austen had been trying to talk with them, and one day he called me and was very frustrated over the recruiter at the local mall basically blowing him off. He and I talked, and I told him to look at it from a different point of view.

I said, "Son, I know you, but they don't. You have to look at it like this. They get paid by the number of guys they recruit. They see you as someone they don't want to waste time on because you are over the weight requirements. I can imagine they probably get quite a few people who just mosey in the door and talk to them without any true intention of joining up. They don't see you as a real possibility for success because of the weight issue. If you want them to pay attention to you, you are going to have to show them you mean business by losing weight. Show them that they are totally wrong in judging you. Make them pay attention to you."

He made up his mind to do just that, and he and I started a journey of working out together, and I coached him on diet. The time I had spent bodybuilding came in handy. We worked out and ran several days per week, and a lot of days, we would go to a local restaurant that had a salad bar, and we would eat together too.

After he had lost a good bit of weight (my memory fails me as to how many pounds, but it was a substantial number), he went back to the recruiter's office. This time, they paid attention, and though he was still a bit over the weight table statistic, they talked to him about signing up, had him complete some forms, and gave him a date by which he needed to be at the proper weight in order to enter the Army. He was happy, but he only had a couple of weeks to lose the last few pounds.

As the final date got closer, he had a week left with about seven or so pounds to lose. He was concerned he wouldn't make it, so I told him I could give him a diet he could follow for a few days that would help him, but he had to promise me that he would only use it the one time because it really wasn't a good diet for a young man to follow, and it was tough as hell to do. He agreed, and the week went by. When he weighed at the recruiting office, he had made the weight. That was one happy young man, and I was happy for him. We had done more than work out together. We had worked through some things together.

When my son got to come home for ten days leave after boot camp, he and Austen and I went to the movies. We went to see the movie *300* together because my son and I had talked about how good the trailer looked. Austen and I had gone to see it already, but we didn't say anything because it was a movie my son expressed interest in, and we were just so happy to be together again. I sat in that movie theater and kept my face averted because of the tears streaming down my face when I saw the wife of Leonides receive the news of her husband's death. Raw emotion. I had lost my own warrior husband too, and it hurt like hell.

I don't believe in coincidences in life. I believe I was meant to see that movie at that time with my boys. I know that it helped me, and Leonides' queen, Gorgo, was a warrior herself. Spartan women, like Gorgo's character, actually did physical training during that time period. The physical and emotional strength portrayed in Gorgo were very moving to me at that moment. It seems that even in the movie theater, my Shadow Warrior had my back.

All three of us walked out of the theater talking, and we found out that my son had already seen the movie too, and we all laughed because we had kept that fact from each other so we could all be together again and see a movie we thought the other one wanted to see. Memories like that sustain me. Just one of the reasons I still love those three boys so much.

Kris didn't get to see the movie with us, but we did things with him when he wasn't working. I remember once, I had a flat tire, and I called Kris. As many things as I had learned from my dad about how to take care of my own vehicle, I never had changed a tire, and I wasn't sure I could do it correctly with the newer, more modern jacks. The old jacks I remembered from when I was younger were much less complicated and a lot stronger, but such is the price of progress. Kris came over and changed my tire for me, no hesitation. There wasn't and still isn't much that boy can't do.

Austen began preparing for Army boot camp, and I began preparing to move from my house because I couldn't pay the mortgage.

∞

My son got to come home again later on leave a few months before he was deployed to Iraq. By then, I had moved and was cleaning houses to make ends meet (I'll come back to that later in the book), and I was overjoyed to see him. He had packed on a lot of muscle from working out with some of the muscle heads in the Marine Corps gym, but he was still my baby boy. Of course, I didn't and don't treat him like a child, but no matter how old they get, they are still our babies.

When I had to take him to the airport after his leave was over, I felt like I had been gut punched again. It seemed I was destined to keep watching my son walk away from me and be far, far away. I had to go clean houses, so I had about a two-hour drive back from the airport in which to get myself together. I cried while I drove. I did that a lot during that time, crying while I drove and thinking while I cleaned.

Cleaning houses was a pretty solitary endeavor because most of the time the customers weren't at home, and I preferred it that way. It is not mindless work, but once a pattern of how to clean each home is set, the mind can take over and think all kinds of thoughts.

The thinking was not always beneficial, but rather a mix of negative thought and worry along with time for reflection on current and past aspects of my life. While my son was deployed to Iraq, I did get a call from him every now and then, but I had a lot of time for praying that he came home all in one piece. Fortunately, he did, but there were some close calls, more than I even know about, I am sure.

One day I received a call from him, and I am glad I was home. I won't give the details of what happened to him out of respect for his privacy because he is a very private person. That is why his name is nowhere to be found in any of my books. He talked to me about a close call with a vehicular accident and how he honestly had no idea how he came out unscathed. We talked for a bit, and he had to go. When I hung up the phone, I fell to my knees in the backyard and lost my shit. Big, racking, ugly sobs of fear and relief that he was all right. It took quite a few minutes for me to get myself together before I could even move. While on my knees, I talked to Billy, God, and my dad, and gave thanks for my son being okay, and asked for help. I was floundering, I was scared, I was broke, and I didn't have a lot of hope. My strut was there. My Shadow Warrior was there too, but the hopelessness and fear had the upper hand for the time being.

HELP FROM THE SHADOW WARRIOR

I rarely think back on those days, but I know that I received support from my Shadow Warrior. She was there, quietly in the background holding me up. As I write this, my imagination brings forth an image of me lying face down on the ground, fingernails digging into the earth, chest heaving with the pain and agony of loss, not feeling I had the strength to go on. There, invisible to me, is my Shadow Warrior standing over me, reaching down to pick me up. This image, a very powerful one represents my Shadow Warrior, my inner self, the place from which my power flows.

7

MOVING THROUGH HEARTBREAK

I HAD TO SWALLOW MY PRIDE and ask for help. My
life was in ruins, and my finances were a disaster. I
couldn't live where I had made my home with Billy
after he passed away. There weren't overwhelming
medical bills, just a few because of Billy's insurance.
I simply couldn't pay the mortgage and household
living expenses on one salary. I had left the legal
office in December 2006 as Billy's condition
worsened. Even forcing myself to go back to the
legal office wouldn't have been enough; even if I
had chosen that for myself, I couldn't face being
miserable every day in that office environment.

My "son" Austen went into boot camp with the
Army. It was his mom, Sharon, that I went to for
help. I want to talk about Sharon here. She is a
warrior herself, as I always appreciated how she
stood beside me on the figurative battleground of
life, ready to fight as I navigated tough moments.

She is a faithful Christian and tolerant of my language and mannerisms. She helped me through some of the hardest days of my life and never ever asked for anything in return. She has lived through some very hard times in her life, as well, but she still has a pure soul and a trusting nature. Her naivete about some things is quite endearing. An occurrence during one of our yard sales in which I was selling off many of my possessions demonstrates her purity and my raucous personality.

One of the Saturdays we were doing a yard sale, she and I were sitting out on the driveway waiting for shoppers. It was early because anyone who knows anything about yard sales knows they must begin early. As we sat there in my neighborhood, we saw a car pull into the driveway of one house across and over from mine. A couple got out of the car and started making out. The guy pushed the girl against the car, and the carnal episode began.

We didn't think a lot of it at first, but as things progressed, the guy unzipped his pants and pushed them down to his thighs. Sharon was abashed, and I started laughing. After all, that is my personality. He must have heard me laughing, so he opened the car door, and they fell into the back seat. No modesty there, for sure. I was laughing my ass off, and Sharon laughed too, but she was more shocked than anything else. The look on her face made me laugh even harder, not at her, but at the raw audacity of it. Here we were, two women friends selling the remains of my life so I could try to crawl my way out of a deep, black hole, and the Universe saw fit to send some humor my way. Our Shadow Warriors work in mysterious ways. They are helpers from the Universe that reside within to help us in various moments. Considering the time it took for the couple to complete the rendezvous, it was a reasonable assumption that he was not interested in a long-term goal. They finished, and he walked her to the door; she went in, and he left. I had seen a lot in my time, but that was a first. Sharon and I still laugh about that sometimes. I did wonder, and I still do, if that young woman was allowing that to happen because she felt unworthy of a better relationship. I hope that somewhere down the road, her own Shadow Warrior rose up and showed her that she is worthy of much better treatment than that.

It took more than one yard sale, but I eventually sold everything I could that was of any value and packed up everything else. It took quite a while, but with Sharon's help, I got it done. I rented a U-Haul truck, and Danny, her husband, drove it and followed me as I drove the truck Billy and I had bought for my son in high school. I didn't have our vehicles anymore. I had to turn them back in because I couldn't make the payments. The only vehicle I had left was that beautiful old Chevy truck that my son loved because he loved old trucks. I have always loved old trucks too, and driving it made me feel connected to my son and Billy.

I moved from South Carolina to North Carolina, leaving forty years of life behind, heading into a new era in my life. I had to move in with my mother; otherwise, I would have been homeless, and both she and my sister lived in North Carolina. I was forty-six years old. I wasn't full of hope. I was full of grief, despair, and fear. I had lost my material possessions, but more importantly, I had lost the love of my life, and my son was far away.

My mom and I lived in a very old, two-story house on a dead-end street in Rutherfordton, North Carolina. The neighbors were okay, and the house was pretty old. We were renting, so it wasn't a nice home, but it was a roof over our heads.

When Danny, Sharon, and I got to the old two-story house, we started moving furniture. I had a lazy boy recliner and reclining sofa that Billy and I had bought together early on in our marriage. I couldn't part with them even though they were really too big for the small rooms in that old house alongside my mother's furniture.

That couch was nearly the death of us! We had to take that couch in the front door, a narrow front door, then down the small hallway that had a set of stairs on one side, making it an even tighter fit. That wasn't even the hard part. At the end of that small, narrow hallway, we had to make a turn into the room I was going to put the couch into, and the turn was almost ninety degrees. That isn't all. There was a wall in front of us, the doorway to the room was to the right, and the hallway made a hard right turn just past the wall.

We twisted and turned and finally got part of the couch into the room, but there was no room to slide by to get inside and finish pulling the couch into the room. We stood and looked at it for a moment. We had turned the couch so that it was angled, creating a space between the seat and the armrest, and this space was up against the doorway of the room we needed to get into. I stood for a moment more, then I wiggled through the space into the room and pulled while Danny and Sharon pushed. We finally got it through, but boy was it an episode for a comedy show. We still laugh about that day too.

We got all the things unpacked that day, but I had more to do. I drove the U-Haul myself later and brought some more things. I had a hand truck I was using, and I don't even remember what I was unloading, but I remember the small concrete front porch of that house was slick from the morning dew that day, and my foot slipped, and I landed flat on my back on that porch. My first thought was that I hoped none of the neighbors saw me because those old voices that called me stupid were loud. I laid there for a moment, only because it hurt like hell, but I got up and finished the job. In those days, when something like that occurred, I felt like I deserved it.

That was something I had to overcome. It is not uncommon for impoverished people to believe that they deserve their circumstances. People can live below the poverty line for any number of reasons, but our culture looks down on them. No one looked down on me as hard as I did myself.

Whether we want to admit it or not, we judge others, especially if they are considered low income. In our minds, we think that the people are poor because they don't handle money well, or they are too lazy to work, or whatever other stupid reason the system has invented. Our society also has a tendency to believe that wealthy people should share their wealth or otherwise be viewed as greedy and uncaring. These are all beliefs that serve no one, and it took a long time for me to recognize what I was doing to myself by believing and perpetuating the stereotype.

I drove back and forth to South Carolina to work the job I had gotten at a Merry Maids franchise for a while, but the money I spent on gas didn't really make the job worthwhile. I got the job with the cleaning company when I lived in South Carolina, for the same reason I called myself stupid when I fell on that porch that morning. I thought I wasn't worthy. I figured I must have done some kind of terrible thing for which I was paying the price, losing my husband, my finances, and my self-worth in what felt like one fell swoop. I didn't believe I could get a decent job anywhere else, even though I had left the police department with an excellent record, and I had experience in two different attorney's offices.

Part of all of this was the grief, I am sure. What I was certain of was that I did not want to work in another damned attorney's office. That was not for me. I was sick of everything and believed in nothing. I was in pain and adrift and had low hopes. My Shadow Warrior was there, the whole time, but I couldn't feel her.

My mom saw an ad in the paper advertising for help at a woman's gym. You may remember I loved going to the gym in South Carolina and had been an amateur bodybuilder. I wasn't in peak bodybuilding shape, but I was still in decent condition, so I called for an interview and got the job. It was part time, and I had begun cleaning houses on my own as well, so I was beginning to make some money. Despite this uptick, the money was still nowhere near enough to recover from and cover all of my bills and debt, and it was going to be a long time before I had a decent credit score again. However, my work at the gym helped to open the pathway of communication with my Shadow Warrior.

The ladies at the gym where I worked helped me through a lot of the kinds of moments like I mentioned earlier with my son being in Iraq. Though I didn't tell them of any incident with particulars, and I didn't break down in front of them, they could tell I was afraid for my son, and they understood. These women were warriors too, and we held each other up. I made some wonderful friends working at that gym, and I still keep in touch with some of them. Once again, I am reminded of that image I often have of the women warriors of ancient times standing side-by-side and going toe to toe with their adversaries.

Two friends in particular were especially helpful to me. These two women were church-going, Christian women with a sense of humor that kept me going. They accepted my language and my mannerisms (much like Sharon) and helped me in so many ways that I don't even have the words to describe it. Though they never used the language I did, they didn't judge me.

We trained together at the gym and sometimes outside of the gym. We talked about life with all of its ups and downs, pain and suffering, and we spoke of the love we had for our families and our children. One of the women had a son too, but he was much younger than mine. It didn't matter, though, because she completely understood my fear and the deep, abiding love I had for my son. The Shadow Warrior brought those women to me. They became my comrades in battle.

HELP FROM THE SHADOW WARRIOR

The gym environment had, once again, provided me with support, friendship, and an outlet for pain by connecting me with these strong, fierce women. I know my Shadow Warrior brought us together, and we learned from each other, but mostly we leaned on each other.

My Shadow Warrior had a difficult job during this time of my life. It was hard for her to communicate with me because I was grief-stricken and feeling very much like a victim of life. I have since healed enough to come to the realization that I am not a victim, and my Shadow Warrior is always there, whether I see her or not. She shows up in many ways, one of which is in friends that help, like Sharon and Danny, and little synchronicities that come about.

When I think about those times and all of the help those two beautiful souls gave me, I envision the ancient women warriors on the battlefields standing side by side facing the enemy. I like to think that Sharon and Danny were two of those fellow comrades that helped me to face down my demons, along with my Shadow Warrior.

8

EARNING A PHD IN HUMAN NATURE

I STARTED WITH a couple of houses per week as I worked at the women's gym in the evenings and on Saturdays. By word of mouth, it wasn't long before I got more clients and was cleaning several houses per week, some weekly, some bi-weekly. I charged fifty dollars per house if I could clean the house in four hours or less. If it took longer than four, I would adjust accordingly.

I had a couple of big houses that took longer, but for the most part, I did my houses in four hours. When I completed the houses for that day, I usually had about an hour, sometimes less, before I had to work at the gym. Normally, I would book two houses per day, but sometimes I had three, and that was tough going.

Cleaning people's houses taught me a great deal more about human nature than I had learned as a cop. Police officers, firefighters, paramedics, nurses, and various other first responders and medical field workers predominantly spend their time with the people in the worst of situations. As a house cleaner—notice I didn't refer to myself as a maid—I saw less immediate crisis, but I still had a front row seat for human nature.

Most of my customers were great, and I had learned from my time with Merry Maids how to start a certain way to clean each room and how to methodically work my way through the entire house systematically. I got a good reputation for doing a good job, and I even picked up extra work sometimes with jobs for my customers beyond their regularly scheduled cleanings.

I also picked up extra work by applying at the community college for a part-time janitorial position working special events at their auditorium. I could do those on the weekends and still keep up my regular customer's houses and the gym job. I basically was working my ass off to try to crawl out of the hole I was living in. At the time, I don't think I gave it much conscious thought, but I knew in my gut what I was doing. I was cleaning physically while my psyche was trying to clean itself of the pain, grief, and feelings of no self-worth I was carrying. My Shadow Warrior stood calmly waiting as I cleaned out the messes, so she could more clearly communicate with me.

I remember one of my customers who was the epitome of Southern ladyhood. She was petite with a cute little figure, makeup always perfect, and the bearing and mannerisms of Southern charm. She had a lovely two-story home, and I never minded cleaning her house because it was so wonderfully neat and clean already. She was always kind and considerate of me, and despite the fact that she had money, she didn't treat me like I was a servant. She always treated me as a person, though through no fault of hers, I still felt the chasm of social classes.

Another customer became a good friend. She was a psychiatric nurse and was so pretty and funny. I loved her little cabin in the woods. It was two stories and so cute in the way they had remodeled it. She and her partner (she didn't want to get married) lived there, and he was friendly and likable. When they went out of town, I would house sit for them and take care of their dog. I have always loved dogs, so this was right up my alley. Years after I left my cleaning business, I heard that the dog had died, and it broke my heart. He was the sweetest dog ever.

Sometimes, I would get inquiries from referrals from my regular customers. I got a call from a man who owned apartment buildings and constructed houses, so I took on cleaning jobs for his properties sometimes too. I didn't like working for him very much because he didn't want to pay my price, and my price was quite reasonable. I remember one apartment I had to clean for him, and it was one of those that made me wish to hell I'd never gotten involved in cleaning.

The bathroom was so nasty it took forever for me to make it presentable, but that was nothing compared to the mess I found on the cooking range. When I pulled the range out from its spacing to survey the overall look of it, I found stains all down the sides from what appeared to be more than one cooking disaster, and none of them were recent. These were deep, crusty, thick stains that looked like more than one spill had been left to cement themselves to the side of the stove that was invisible when it was in place beside the kitchen cabinet. I spent hours just on that damned stove, and still had the rest of the apartment to clean.

Later, after I had finished cleaning that piece of shit and gone home, I received a call from the owner complaining to me because he had opened a drawer in the kitchen that had items in it. When I went by to see what he was talking about and he pulled the drawer out, it wasn't anything nasty, just a couple of items left behind like a notepad and a screwdriver, or something like that. No acknowledgment of how much better the apartment looked, just a complaint about a drawer. I know I missed the damned drawer, but he didn't care how hard it had been to clean that disgusting apartment, yet he said it had embarrassed him when he was showing the apartment and he found the drawer wasn't empty. I wanted to tell him he had no idea what it felt like to be really embarrassed, but I didn't. If something like that happened today, since my Shadow Warrior and I have become in sync, I would tell the bastard to fuck off.

The money wasn't worth it, so the next time he called, I told him I couldn't do the job. I was starting to get myself back. I was slowly beginning to allow my long-buried strut to come out and push back. I was beginning to listen to my Shadow Warrior, see my true value, and recognize that just because I had lost so much didn't mean I wasn't a worthy human being.

I had another client with a huge house I cleaned every two weeks. Both she and her husband were doctors, and they owned a three-story house that took me between six and seven hours to clean. She was nice, but I felt the distance of class hierarchy. I had gotten used to it, to a degree. Her husband was a cool cat and funny. I had heard people in the community talk about him in a very positive way. They had three children at home, one of whom was a teenaged boy, and his room looked like a mini Chernobyl every time I cleaned.

Usually, no one was home when I cleaned, which is the way I preferred it because people in the house have a tendency to get in the way. The husband was home for a little while one day, and he was in the downstairs office, well out of the way. I had begun working on the son's room when I heard the doctor come upstairs. He stopped at his son's bedroom door and said, "If I were you, I would refuse to clean this room." I smiled and chuckled because what could I say that would be acceptable. What I said in my head was, *That's easy for you to say, and though I appreciate the thought, your wife hired me, so I am pretty sure she would fire me.* I didn't need to lose that house because it was one of the two that I made the most money on.

Their home was beautiful, but it was a bear to clean, just because of the size. It was three full floors. The only room in the house that was really dirty was the son's bedroom and bathroom. Each floor of the home had enough space for a family to live on each of them.

The basement held a full bathroom, two sets of bunk beds, a pool table, and a full home theater setup. I always cleaned the basement last because I began on the top floor and worked my way down, so by the time I reached it, many negative thoughts were swirling in my head. I had thoughts like,"These people have enough room for several families to live in, and they pay someone to clean up after them. It must be nice to have this much money. Rich folks have no understanding of what it's like to live hand to mouth." I know now that those are all beliefs that don't serve me. I also know that we all have a chance for success, despite what our cultural background consists of. Those days were a learning ground for me, and I know I needed to go through them to get better. My Shadow Warrior was there. She never left me, but my negative thoughts and feelings of low self-worth and self-pity sometimes drowned her out.

The bathroom of the basement usually didn't take very long because no one used the tub and shower on a regular basis, but occasionally, it was evident the kids had entertained friends overnight. I remember thinking I could live in that basement and have plenty of room, but then I would tell myself it was my fault I was where I was financially and otherwise, and I would chastise myself for the self-pity. I was a psychological mess for sure.

Working alone, instead of for a cleaning company, was much better for me, especially during that time. I used the drive between houses as a source of peace. A couple of the places I cleaned were in the mountains about thirty to forty minutes from my home, so I had some good thinking time, and the view was beautiful.

The houses I cleaned in the mountains were in a resort, and they were lovely. The people were pretty nice, but I could feel the classism heavily in those two places. My old Ford Ranger pickup fit in with the other contractors who made their living serving the privileged resort residents.

One older couple lived in a cute, little place on the lake. The lady had Parkinson's disease, and their bathroom always took me a while. It was a pretty bathroom with a nice garden tub, but there were cosmetics containers and bottles and various other grooming and medicinal paraphernalia that needed to be removed before I could clean. I could really say that about the whole cabin. There was stuff everywhere. It wasn't like a hoarder's place, but more so like they downsized from their previous home and tried to keep all of their belongings in this smaller home. However, they were kind and polite and added tips to my pay pretty frequently.

As I would leave the resort on those days I cleaned, I would look out across the scenery and think about the beauty of it. I would also think about how much I would like to own my own house again, but at that time, I felt it was a long way away, if I ever reached that point again. I would shake the thought off and move on to the next job.

In addition to cleaning houses, working as a janitor for the community college and working at the gym, I started bartending on the weekends. I finished my evenings at the gym on Fridays by 9:00 p.m., and I would go work at the bar, but I spent the most time bartending on Saturdays and Sundays, so I was working seven days per week for a while

Bartending, like cleaning, is a study in human nature. In both occupations, people's secrets became apparent when I was observant. When cleaning a home, though it may not be intentional, I could tell things about the owners by what they left lying around or what they valued more by what they wanted my cleaning focus to be. I have had customers who wanted more attention on things like a shiny kitchen floor, yet they didn't mind so much the mold growing in the bathroom tiles enough to put a fan blowing on the shower stall after they had showered, to dry it more quickly. With bartending, people revealed their secrets when they drank too much because alcohol reduces inhibitions. However, the tips could be pretty decent, and I needed the extra income to buy a new set of tires for my truck.

That little truck was a good one. It was old, but it ran like a top. The most embarrassing thing about that truck was the credit box attached. This was an apparatus attached to the vehicle so that if a payment was missed, the vehicle would not start. My credit was shit because of the economic devastation I was experiencing from losing Billy, my house, and a lot more. Seeing people spend as much money at the bar as they did used to make me wonder what they were thinking because I knew some of them, and they all weren't rich. I guess a lot of them were trying to numb the pain, the pain of poverty, apathy, drug addiction, or just life in general. Whatever their reasons, I noticed their pain, and I recognized it because I lived in the area and saw the struggles every day. I saw people abusing their spouses and children, living on the poverty line with the constant awareness that a lay-off or business shut down would result in complete devastation. I recognized it because I was living it, so I knew that drinking was a means of forgetting for a time, forgetting the hardships and constant struggles of their lives.

We all numb our pain in many ways. I indulged in alcohol-related numbing many times during this painful time dealing with the loss of Billy and my son fighting in a war far away from home. I was in pain for these reasons and more, so I could understand the how and why of some of the bar patrons. It is easy to fall into a deep hole filled with hopelessness and doubt. Many of the people in the bar were struggling with the same kinds of things I was, like the credit box. I am sure they all felt varying degrees of worthlessness and shame, similar to how I felt. Our culture treats poverty as a contagious disease.

I never let anyone know about the credit box. It is difficult to write about these things because of the stigma placed on people who live in poverty. I never had to go on welfare assistance, but if I hadn't had my mother helping, I don't know where I would have ended up. Of course, I had friends, but I was raised with the mindset that you didn't ask people, especially friends, for money. It is a pride thing too. I lived in a fog of pain, poverty, and fear for years, never hearing the cry of the Shadow Warrior trying to get me to listen.

In my current teaching position, I encounter many students I know are experiencing poverty with all of its food insecurities and other things associated with economic oppression. Sometimes I remind myself that these students may not have the emotional support I had, and they may have even more to overcome than I did.

While I was cleaning and doing the other jobs, I tried dating. It was a disaster, and it didn't take a very long time for me to wake up and realize I was comparing every man I met with Billy, and as I stated before, none would ever measure up. When I realized this, I felt freer. I decided to accept this and just focus on rebuilding my life as a single woman. I am glad I did.

It took a while for me to realize that what I needed was to prove to myself that I could stand on my own two feet. I made it, and I am glad I made the decision to stay single. To this day, I don't lament over not having a romantic partner. I sometimes think of my grandmother and compare myself to her. My grandmother (my mom's mom) lost her husband when she was thirty-nine years old. He died of an aneurysm, leaving her with several children out of a total of ten still at home. My mother says my grandma used to ask what man would want a woman with that many kids, but I suspect she just didn't have the energy to try another marriage, and it would have had to be a marriage because of her moral compass. While I may have more progressive views of relationships, I think I felt a similar tug as my grandmother to simply live my life as a single woman.

HELP FROM THE SHADOW WARRIOR

The funny thing about recognizing my Shadow Warrior and claiming my strut is knowing that during all of this time of terrible pain, I was never alone. I always had the Shadow Warrior in the background supporting me, holding me up, pushing me forward. Even though I wasn't consciously aware of her during many of the hard times, I believe that deep inside, some part of me recognized she was there, and that subconscious knowing supported me through those truly horrific times.

9

A NEW BEGINNING:
A NEW CAREER

WHILE I WAS WORKING at the ladies gym, one of the members came in, and we started talking. She was the nicest person, and over time, we got to know each other. She worked for an association that helped people who wanted to change career paths. She helped me enroll in her program that provided me with financial assistance to attend the local community college. I couldn't believe I was going to be able to afford to return to college. This was just one of the serendipities that occurred to help me. I know now that it was my Shadow Warrior helping me out.

The day I went to register for college, I met the woman who would be my first English instructor there, and who I am still friends with today. She gave me a lot of encouragement, and she knows that I credit her with my subsequent English degree. I had always done well in English, and as I wrote about in my first book, I had buried my secret desire to be a writer, a desire I'd had since I was around ten years old.

The college had an essay contest, and she helped me with my entry by giving me feedback and advice. That really paid off because I won second place, and my essay was published in the school literary magazine. That was the spark that ignited that low burning fire I had since I was young. It was another gift from my Shadow Warrior.

I completed my two years at the community college and transferred to a private university not too far from home. I received a lot of help at the community college, and I met some wonderful folks who are still my friends. I made good grades and worked my butt off so that I could graduate and transfer to a university for a four-year degree.

While I attended community college, I still cleaned houses and worked at the gym. After a while, I was able to leave cleaning, and boy was I glad. I had a couple of my customers who had become friends say they were glad I was pursuing my degree but were sad that I was leaving. One of my customers had often asked me why I didn't branch out to a bigger cleaning business. I told her I didn't want to do that because hiring people could be fraught with difficulties I didn't want to manage, but deep down, I knew I didn't want to clean houses for the rest of my life.

The community college had an articulation agreement with the private university, and though it may sound like it was more expensive than attending a state supported school, it afforded me the opportunity to continue to pursue my undergraduate degree and still work my jobs. It was only about a twenty-minute drive from home, so I could still work and attend classes.

I had to learn more than just the material for my classes. I had to master the digital environment. When I worked in the second attorney's office, we were just going to Microsoft Windows and hooking up to the internet. The office manager's husband was employed as an IT guy, so he gave us lessons on how to navigate the computer, but by no means was I completely comfortable with it. I signed up for as many in-person courses as I could manage and still work until I learned how to navigate the digital environment more comfortably.

At the private university I attended, I met many amazing folks who also came to be my friends. I felt the difference in being a nontraditional student there more so than at the community college, for I was definitely in the minority as far as older students are concerned. I felt out of place much of the time, but I felt my inner warrior getting stronger as I began regaining my power, and I pushed on.

Most of the time, the students were friendly, and many of them told me how funny they thought I was. They didn't realize how out of place I felt, and not just because of my age. I was wrestling those demons of low self-esteem and shame because of living below the poverty line. I wasn't nearly as bad off as many people. I know this, but I can still understand how awful it feels to not know whether or not there will be enough money to pay for everything that must be paid, or to not have any money to buy lunch or a cup of coffee. It was embarrassing, especially when there wasn't enough money to buy the textbooks.

Fortunately, the students also didn't know some of the things that would go through my mind when I sat there in class listening. I had been on the street. I had seen things because of what I had done for a living and just simply because of my age. I would sit there thinking, *Damn, was I ever that young and naive?* I was older than most of the professors and had those same thoughts about them as well, but I still respected them. They all helped me a lot.

In the end, I finished my undergraduate degree and planned to get a master's degree. As I was looking around to find a university for the master's degree, I was talking with the brilliant woman who had mentored me through my senior English project and found that I could do a graduate assistant position in the writing center at this university and offset some of the costs of the tuition for my master's degree. That was good news and one of the best things that ever happened. Our friendship is one I most cherish these days.

While I worked as a graduate assistant for the writing center at the small private university, I was teaching academic development courses at the community college I had previously attended. As a result, my financial situation began to improve, slowly but surely. I was still dealing with the feelings of "not enough," but my Shadow Warrior was reminding me that I still had the strut.

When I graduated with that master's degree, my two friends from the gym attended the ceremony. That is real friendship because those ceremonies are boring. Once again, my platoon of women warriors stood alongside me as I prepared for my new career as an English teacher.

HELP FROM THE SHADOW WARRIOR

There were many, many times I felt the shame of poverty and loss as I made my way through the educational minefield. My Shadow Warrior, once again, sent me some powerful comrades to stand with me as I faced new challenges. During this period of my life, I imagine myself a battle-weary warrior going through rehabilitation from an injury. My comrades helped me build my strength back up through encouragement and mentoring. My Shadow Warrior chose the right ones for this task, and she threw me some new challenges to face to remind me of what I was made of: strength, resilience, power, and a heavy dose of kick-ass attitude.

10

HELP, WINNING OVER DOUBT, AND RECOGNIZING THE SILENT STRUT OF MY SHADOW WARRIOR

ONE THING I LEARNED over the years and through the obstacles and pain is that there are a lot of people who are willing to help. It sounds rather dense of me to write it like that, but the thing is, I had been raised to believe that asking for help from people outside the family, and even some in the family, was something you avoided so that you wouldn't be "beholden" to them and have to reciprocate.

Maybe that really wasn't what my parents intended, but it was most definitely the message I received, and I think it came from the social hierarchy they observed. In other words, "other" people would look down on us because we came from poor folks, and our people weren't educated, rich, or whatever, etc.

A valuable lesson to learn in life is that none of us can live without help at some point in our lives, and there is no shame in asking for help. Being independent is fine, but there are times in everyone's life when they need help. I recognize now that the mindset my parents had was a product of their own upbringing, and they weren't the only ones who thought this way. I also recognize that judgment is a big influencer in many people's lives, especially those who are not financially stable. Because people who live from paycheck to paycheck feel and are judged, they reciprocate by judging in return, so we have this circle of judgment that never ends.

I felt my own judgment like a heavy weight I carried all the time, and I would wager a guess that my own judgment was most probably worse than any I was imagining or receiving. Most of the time, people are too busy with their own lives to spend a lot of time thinking about others, and the judgment syndrome, along with an inferiority complex, is actually rather arrogant, and I have spent a lot of time in that arrogance arena. However, I do recognize that a warrior needs a certain amount of arrogance to get through things in life. When I visualize my Shadow Warrior strutting her power, I see arrogance that drives her through the obstacles in her way.

How we approach our lives directly affects how things will turn out. I am a firm believer in the idea that we are all masters of our destiny. I don't mean this to say that those who suffer from abuse and neglect, especially children, have brought that type of thing to themselves, but I do mean that we have the capacity to rise up and make changes and chase dreams.

I still fall into old thought and belief patterns, just like anyone else. After a time, however, I realize that I am repeating an old pattern and instead, remind myself of what I have accomplished. We humans, and especially women, are discouraged from asserting our awesomeness because it is viewed as conceit or being "stuck-up," and I heard those falsehoods my entire life. These views are bullshit and another tool of a culture that seeks to oppress anyone in any marginalized group. We need to recognize the powerful strut of the Shadow Warrior and let her assert herself in our lives.

I realize that I have the privilege of being a white woman. I understand that as a white woman, I have no idea what it feels like to be a part of certain marginalized groups, whether based upon race, ethnicity, disability, etc. I do, however, believe that any breakthroughs I can make for and with women will assist other groups in breaking through collectively.

There are many stories of humans from various backgrounds and cultures who have broken through the obstacles placed in their way and succeeded. It is my belief that if a human has done something, that means it is humanly possible. I am a human, so that means I can do the seemingly impossible too. This "anything is possible" is a philosophy that I hold onto. I even used this philosophy when my "son" Austen and I were training together so he could meet the army's weight requirements. I have told my students in my classes this same philosophy.

Every human, regardless of gender has the right to live their lives freely and to pursue their dreams without sanction as long as we do no harm to others. This is my belief, and this is what I hope women will take away from my book. We are warriors, and we are free. Let the Shadow Warrior strut on.

My dear reader, I hope that you have been able to envision the Shadow Warrior that resides within you as you have read this book. I hope that you have felt that pull to recognize who you are and what you are capable of. I hope that you find more encouragement and power than you have ever known. This is my wish for you, and I acknowledge you and your Shadow Warrior with a loud, hearty battle cry. Hear it now in your heart and mind. Strut on!

ACKNOWLEDGMENTS

I HAVE SO MANY PEOPLE to thank for this book that it would take almost another book to name them all, but I would like to mention some here and ask for grace for any I forget.

I would like to thank my ride-or-die fellow woman warrior, Margo Jones. She and I have walked trails and talked, drank coffee and talked, laughed and cried, and been through some difficulties that we were able to maneuver because we leaned on each other. She has heard most of the material that ends up in my books, but she heard it raw and unedited. I have seen her go through losses that would have leveled a weaker woman, but she is still strong and making her way in this world. My friend, you are an inspiration to me, always.

Shana, Cindy, Taylor, Kamesha, and Melisa are the brilliant women of Synergy Publishing Group, and I count them among the most valuable humans in my world. You are all brilliant, strong, and honorable, and I imagine us all standing shoulder-to-shoulder as we face any difficulties in life. I raise my imaginary battle axe and let lose my warrior cry to you.

To my sister, who I still call baby sister, for she is six years younger than I am, I remember the days of carrying you, thinking you were like a beautiful little doll. You were there for me in my darkest hours, calling and checking on me every single day as I faced one of the hardest times of my life. No words are enough to express my thanks to you and my pride in calling you my sister. We share a unique sense of humor that many people don't get, but it is us and that is grand. I see dad in your smile.

My son, the man you have become makes me prouder each day, and that is saying something because I have always been so very proud of you. You are an honorable man with integrity and resilience. Don't ever forget that. You married well, and I am pleased to know that you have the support you need as the two of you continue to build your life together. And my granddaughter, well kiddo, you are precious and don't forget it.

Kris and Austen, I love you as if I birthed you. You are two good men and you should always remember that. Don't let the hard knocks get you down. You are bigger than any hard situations you face.

Mom, you have always been there for us. I honor you in everything you have had to face in your life and I am thankful to have in my corner.

To all the members of my squad, I sure hope you know who you are because I don't have room to write all of your names. I work with some of you—male and female—some of you worked with me in previous years, and we have laughed and bitched and had a blast and I am fortunate to call you friends.

This is not a complete list, but it is demonstrative of how fortunate I am and I hope that this book will touch the lives of any who read it, for that is my goal.

ABOUT THE AUTHOR

Karen Taylor is an English instructor at a local community college near her home in Western North Carolina. She also has a program called *Own Your Strut Squad* that serves as support for women wishing to embrace their power. Her writing explores how women can better understand their inherent power, experience their right to freedom, and find their own strut and their own Shadow Warriors. She is a mother of three sons, one biological, the other two acquired, of which she is fiercely proud. She calls herself humorously inappropriate, and when not writing, she can be found reading books, spending time with her dog and enjoying the beach.

Want to be a part of Karen's Strut Squad?
Contact her at:
karendtaylorstrutsquad@gmail.com
kdtaylor.substack.com
Facebook: Karen Taylor
Instagram: _karen_taylor